JESUS

Is Risen

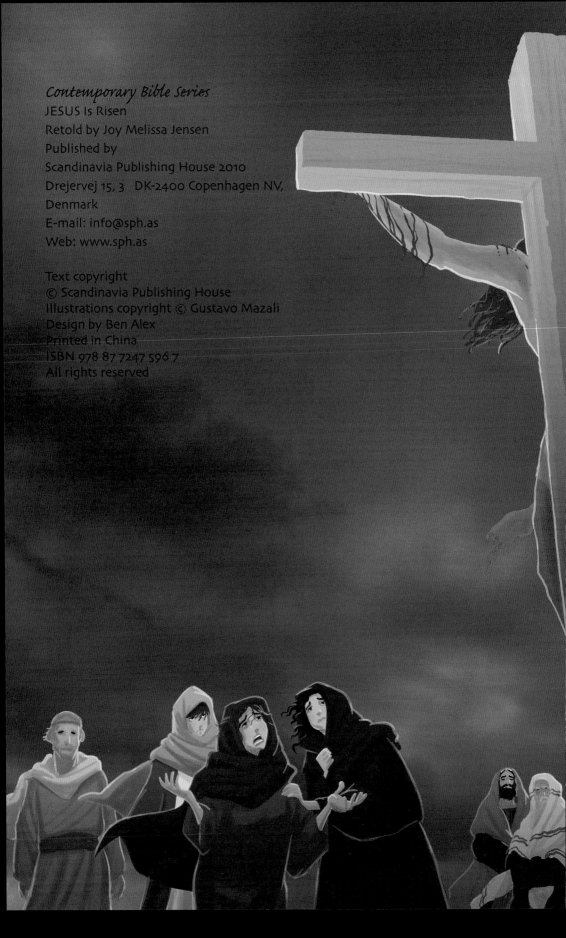

Contemporary Bible Series
JESUS Is Risen
Retold by Joy Melissa Jensen
Published by
Scandinavia Publishing House 2010
Drejervej 15, 3   DK-2400 Copenhagen NV,
Denmark
E-mail: info@sph.as
Web: www.sph.as

Text copyright
© Scandinavia Publishing House
Illustrations copyright © Gustavo Mazali
Design by Ben Alex
Printed in China
ISBN 978 87 7247 596 7

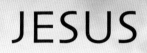

JESUS
Is Risen

Retold for Children

by Joy Melissa Jensen

Scandinavia

Contents

A Special Meal is Prepared
Luke 22:7-13

The day of Passover came. All of Israel woke up early and prepared for the big day. Jesus told Peter and John, "Go make our Passover meal."

"But Jesus," they said, "we have no home where we can cook our food."

"Don't worry about that," said Jesus. "Go into Jerusalem and look for a man with a jar of water. Follow him home. The owner of the house will take you upstairs to a big kitchen. You can make our meal there."

So Peter and John left for Jerusalem. They found a man with a water jar and they followed him back home. Then the owner of the house led them upstairs to a big kitchen. Everything happened just as Jesus said. They made the meal and then went back to Jesus.

5

A New Command

John 13: 31-35

Jesus told his disciples, "I will have to leave you all soon. You will look for me, but I won't be there. God is going to bring glory to his Son! My time has come to go and be with my Father.

But I will leave you with a new command. My command is that you love each other just as I have loved you. If you do as I say, then I will know that you are truly my followers."

The Leaders Shall Serve

Luke 22:14, 24-30

Jesus and his disciples sat down to eat the Passover meal. While they were talking, one of them asked, "Who is the greatest among God's people?" All the disciples had a different opinion. They began to argue. Jesus told them, "Some of you may think a ruler is the greatest because he orders people around. But don't be like that. The greatest person is the one who serves others. I have been a servant to you. Soon I will be gone. If you can serve others as I have served you, then you be with me in my kingdom. Each of you will have a throne, and you will eat and drink at my table."

Jesus Washes the Disciples' Feet

John 13:1-9

The disciples were all sitting around the table. But Jesus stood up. He took off his robe and wrapped a towel around his waist. Then he filled a bowl with water and went back to the table. He knelt down at the disciple's feet and began to wash them. Then he dried them with the towel. The disciples were speechless. But Simon Peter spoke up. He said, "Lord, why are you washing our feet?"

"You don't understand right now, but you will soon," Jesus answered.
Peter didn't want the Lord to do something only a slave would do. He said, "Jesus I won't let you wash my feet."

But Jesus told him, "If I don't wash your feet, then you don't belong to me."

So Peter let him wash his feet along with the other disciples.

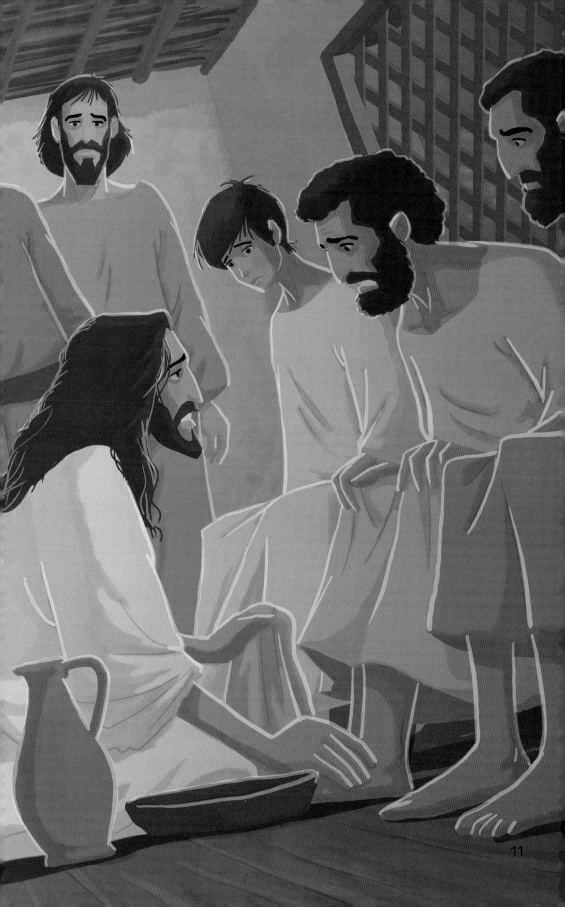

Jesus Sets the Example

John 13:12-17

After Jesus had finished washing the disciples' feet, he sat back down. "Do you know why I have done this?" he asked them. But the disciples were silent. "You call me Lord and that is what I am! I have served you by washing your feet. This is to show you that the most important one should be like the least important. Learn from my example and serve one another. I love you to the very end, and I am willing to do anything for you. Do the same for each other. Now that you know these things, God will bless you if you do them."

The Lord's Supper

Mark 14:18-25

Jesus told his disciples, "One of you dining with me is going to betray me." The disciples hung their heads. They felt sad. "Surely you don't mean me?" each of them asked Jesus. "I would never do a thing like that," each of them said. Jesus told them, "One of you twelve will turn your back on me. I will die and go to the Father. But the man who betrays me will feel terrible. He will wish he had never been born. Then Jesus picked up the loaf of bread from the table. He said a blessing and then broke the bread in two. "Take this bread and eat it," Jesus told them. "It is my body." Then Jesus passed around the wine. "Take this wine and drink it. It is my blood." So the disciples ate and drank. Jesus told them, "I will give up my body for you so that your sins may be forgiven."

15

Peter Will Deny Jesus

Mark 14:26-31

The disciples finished their meal. They sang a hymn and left to find a place to relax. They went to the Mount of Olives. While they were there, Jesus told them, "I will die, and each one of you will turn your back on me. You will be scattered and lost like sheep. But this won't be the end. I will come back and lead you again."

"Lord," Peter said, "Even if the others turn their backs on you, I never will."

But Jesus knew the truth. He said, "You will reject me this very night. Before the rooster crows you will say that you don't know me three times." Peter didn't believe him. "No, I will never do that," he replied. All the other disciples said the same thing.

A Home in Heaven

John 14:1-6

The disciples felt sad and Jesus' could see it in their faces. So he told them, "Don't worry! Just have faith in God, and have faith in his Son too. It's true that I cannot stay with you. But there are many rooms in God's house. I am going ahead of you to prepare a place where we can be together. I wouldn't tell you this if it weren't true."

"Lord," the disciple Thomas replied, "we don't know where you're going. How can we follow you if we don't know the way?"

Jesus told him, "I am the way, the truth and the life! The only way to my Father is through me."

Jesus Prays for His Followers

John 17:1-18:1

After Jesus finished speaking with his disciples, he went off to pray by himself. "Father, you have given me many followers. They have believed in me. They know that I am your Son. Now I am coming home to you, but help my followers who are still in the world. Protect them by your power, and bring them closer to your Word. Keep them safe. I also pray for those who will believe in me through their message. Let them be as one people the way the Father and Son are one that the world may believe that you have sent me."

Jesus finished his prayer and went with his disciples into the garden of Gethsemane.

The Disciples Fall Asleep

Mark 14:33-42

Jesus felt sad and lonely. He knew that he was going to die soon. "Will you stay awake and pray with me?" he asked his disciples. Then he walked a few steps away and knelt in the grass. "Father," he prayed, "I am suffering. You can do anything, so don't let this happen to me. But you must do what you want, and not what I want."

Jesus went back over to his disciples. They had all fallen asleep. This made Jesus feel lonelier than ever. He said to Peter, "Can't you stay awake with me for one hour?" But they couldn't keep their eyes open.

They just mumbled and fell asleep again. So Jesus prayed by himself. When he was finished, he went back to the disciples.

"Aren't you through with resting?" he said to them. "Wake up! It's time for me to be taken away from you. The one who has betrayed me is already coming this way into the garden." The disciples looked around and wondered what Jesus was talking about.

23

Betrayed With a Kiss

John 18:2-8; Matthew 26:48-49

Judas Iscariot told the Roman soldiers where they could find Jesus. "He will be in the garden with the disciples," Judas told the men. "And you will know who

Jesus is because I'll give him a kiss on the cheek." The plan was settled. They lit their torches and carried their weapons. Then they followed Judas to the garden of Gethsemane.

Jesus saw them coming. "Who are you looking for?" he asked them.

"We've come to arrest Jesus," they answered.

"I am Jesus," he said. The soldiers seemed surprised, and they stumbled backwards. So Jesus asked them again, "Who are you looking for?"

"We've come for Jesus," they answered.

"Leave my disciples alone. I am the one you want," Jesus said. Then Judas walked up to Jesus and kissed him on the cheek. The soldiers tied up Jesus' wrist and started to take him away.

Jesus is Taken Away

John 18:10-11; Luke 22:51-53

Peter burned with anger. He wanted to save Jesus. So he pulled out a sword and swung it at the priest's servant. He chopped off his ear, but Jesus stopped him before he could do any more and said, "Put that weapon away, Peter." He touched the servant's ear and made it whole again. Then he turned to the soldiers and the police who had come to arrest him. "Why are you treating me like a criminal? You have come with swords and clubs. Once, we worshiped together in the temple. You never wanted to hurt me then. But I know that this is your time. You don't understand what you are doing. There's a darkness covering your eyes, and you can't see the truth."

Peter's Denial

John 18:12-14, Luke 22:54-62

Jesus was taken to the high priest's house. Peter tried to go with him, but he had to wait outside. Some people had made a fire in the courtyard. Peter went over and sat down next to it. "Aren't you the man who came with Jesus?" a servant girl asked him.

"No, I don't even know him," Peter replied.

A little while later someone else said, "You are Jesus' disciple!"

But Peter said, "No I'm not."

"You must be with Jesus," another man said. "You come from Galilee just like he does."

"I don't know what you're talking about," Peter growled.

Then in the distance a rooster crowed two times. Peter remembered what the Lord had said: "You will deny me three times before the rooster crows."

Peter knew Jesus had been right all along. He felt so bad that he couldn't stop crying.

Jesus is Questioned

Mark 14:53 -65, 15:1

The high priest met with the leaders of Israel. "What has Jesus done?" he asked them. "He's a liar!" they shouted. "He told us he would tear down our temple and rebuild it in three days."

The priest turned to Jesus and said, "Why don't you speak up for yourself?"

But Jesus didn't say a word.

"Are you the Son of God?" the priest asked him.

"Yes, I am!" Jesus answered. "And soon I will be with my Father in heaven."

The priest turned to the leaders. "Aha!" he exclaimed. "Did you hear him say he was God? That's reason enough to kill Jesus." They blindfolded Jesus and tied him up with rope. They beat him and spit in his eyes. Then they took him to Pilate.

Jesus is Sent to Herod

Luke 23:7-12

Pilate did not want to deal with Jesus. He decided to let another ruler judge him. So the soldiers took Jesus to King Herod. Herod was very curious about him. He had heard many stories about Jesus' miracles and wonders. He wanted to see if Jesus could do them again. But Jesus did not do anything for Herod. He didn't even speak. "What is your crime, Jesus?" Herod asked him. Jesus

didn't say a word, so some of the leaders spoke up instead. "He thinks he's the Son of God!" they shouted. Herod sneered at Jesus, "So you think you're God? Well then we'd better put you in some better clothes!" He brought out a fancy robe and put it on Jesus. Herod's soldiers snorted with laughter. They made fun of Jesus for a long time. Finally Herod said, "Send him back to Pilate. I have no reason to kill Jesus."

Pilate Tries to Free Jesus

John 18:28-40

Jesus was led back to Pilate's palace. There was a huge crowd that had gathered outside Pilate's door. They had come to rally against Jesus. "Why are you so angry?" Pilate asked the people. "What has Jesus done wrong?" The mob began to shout all kinds of lies about Jesus. Pilate could hardly understand what they were saying, so he asked, "Why don't you punish him?" But the people cried back, "It's against the law for us to crucify him. We need you to do it!" So Pilate went back inside to Jesus. "Are you the king of the Jews?" he asked him. "Do you believe I am?" Jesus replied.

"The people are saying that you call yourself a king," Pilate said.

"My kingdom does not belong to this world," Jesus replied. "If it were, the people would have stayed true to me."

"So," Pilate said, "you admit to being a king!"

"It's you who say I am a king," Jesus replied. "I was born to tell the truth."

Pilate was frustrated. He didn't want to kill Jesus, but the mob was growing angrier every minute. He went out to them and said, "Jesus doesn't seem guilty. And after all, it's Passover today. Why don't I set him free?"

The mob yelled back, "No! Nail him to a cross!"

38

Jesus is Sentenced to Death

John 19:1-16

Pilate tried to calm the mob. But more and more people kept shouting and crowding around his door. "Tie Jesus up, and we'll whip him," Pilate told his soldiers. "That should make the people happy." So they whipped Jesus and put a crown of thorns on his head. But the people were not satisfied. "Crucify him! Crucify him!" they chanted.

Pilate went over to Jesus. "Where do you come from?" he asked. But Jesus was silent. "Why don't you answer me? Don't you know I have the power to free you?"

Jesus lifted his wearied head and replied, "Only God has the power to free me. Without Him, you couldn't do anything at all to me."

Pilate asked the mob again, "So, you really want me to kill your king?"

"He's not our king," the people yelled back. "Only the Emperor is king."

Pilate finally gave in and handed Jesus over to be killed.

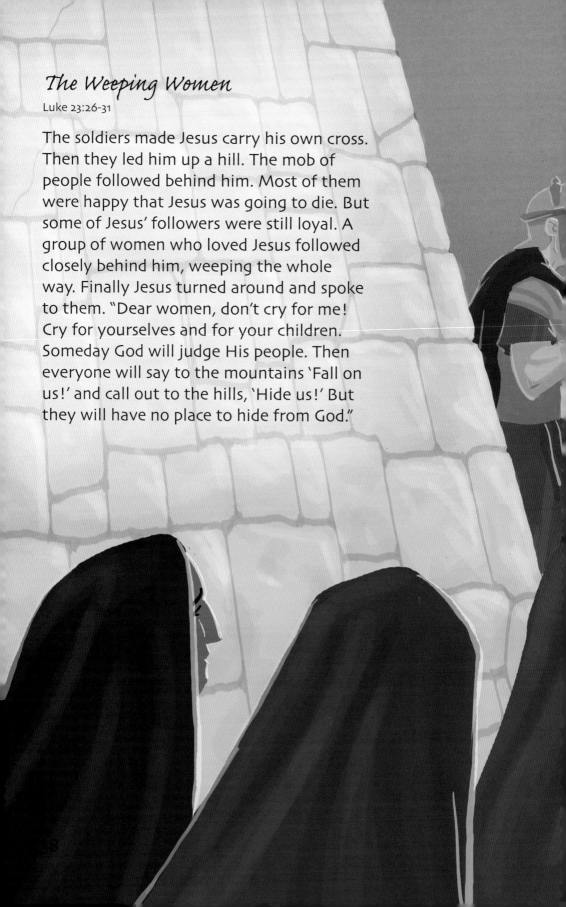

The Weeping Women
Luke 23:26-31

The soldiers made Jesus carry his own cross. Then they led him up a hill. The mob of people followed behind him. Most of them were happy that Jesus was going to die. But some of Jesus' followers were still loyal. A group of women who loved Jesus followed closely behind him, weeping the whole way. Finally Jesus turned around and spoke to them. "Dear women, don't cry for me! Cry for yourselves and for your children. Someday God will judge His people. Then everyone will say to the mountains 'Fall on us!' and call out to the hills, 'Hide us!' But they will have no place to hide from God."

39

Jesus is Nailed to a Cross
Luke 23:32-38

They nailed Jesus to a cross. There was a sign above his head that read: The King of the Jews.

Then the soldiers crucified two other criminals alongside Jesus. The people watched from down below. Some of them made fun of Jesus and called him names.

"Why can't you save yourself?"
the soldiers taunted him. "I
thought you were the Lord!"
Then they gambled for his
clothes. While Jesus was waiting

to die, he prayed, "Forgive these
people, Father! They don't know
what they're doing."

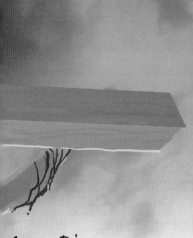

Jesus Dies

Luke 23:39-44; John 19:28-30

One of the criminals who was being crucified said to Jesus, "Aren't you the Lord? Save yourself and save us!" But the other criminal told him, "Don't you fear God? We have been punished for doing wrong. But Jesus is truly innocent." Then he said to Jesus, "Remember me after you die."

Jesus replied, "I promise that you will be with me in heaven." Just then a cloud blocked the sun, and the sky turned dark. Jesus knew his time was almost done. "I'm thirsty!" he said. So someone soaked a sponge with wine. They tied it to a long plant stem and lifted it to Jesus' mouth. He drank from the sponge. Then he said, "Everything is finished!" And he bowed his head and died.

The Earth Trembles

Matthew 27:51-54

The moment Jesus died, the curtain in Jerusalem's temple tore in two. Then an earthquake came and split even the heaviest rocks in two. The graves of Jesus' followers opened up. And when Jesus had risen to life again, his dead followers came up out of their graves to go and see him in Jerusalem. Many of the soldiers and leaders of Israel were scared when all these things happened.

They thought to themselves, "Jesus must have truly been the Son of God!"

44

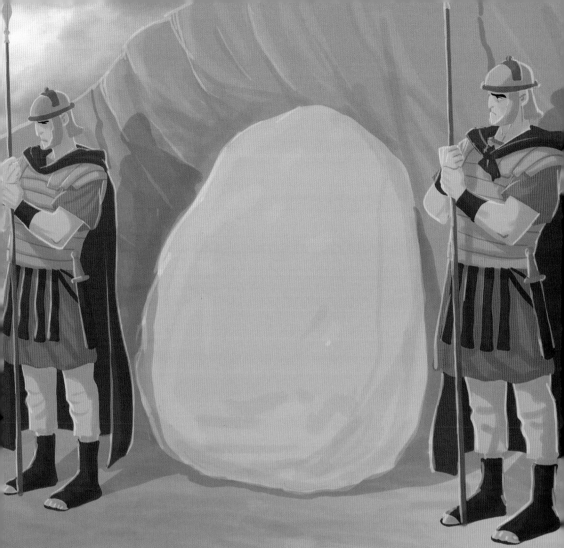

Jesus is Buried

John 19:31-34; Matthew 27:57-61

The next day was a Sunday. The people wanted the bodies to be taken down from the crosses on this special day. So the soldiers took down Jesus' body. But one of Jesus' followers named Joseph came running up to them. He asked the soldiers if he could bury Jesus himself. The soldiers asked Pilate, and Pilate said it was alright. So Joseph took Jesus' body home. He cleaned it and wrapped it in white linen. Then he put him in a tomb that had been cut out from the rocks. He rolled a heavy round stone over the entrance door and left. But two soldiers stayed and guarded the tomb.

47

Jesus Has Risen

Matthew 28:1-10

Mary Magdalene went to
visit Jesus' tomb with the
other Mary. But as soon as
they arrived, an earthquake
rumbled and shook the
ground. The soldiers guarding
the tomb were so frightened
that they both fainted. Then
an angel of the Lord came
down from heaven. His
clothes were bright white,
and his face was shining.
"Don't be afraid," the angel
told the women. "I know
you've come to be with
Jesus. But he isn't here. God
has raised him to life!" The
women were speechless.
They started running back
to town—full of joy and
excitement. They couldn't
wait to tell everybody what
the angel had said. Then
suddenly Jesus came out
and greeted them. "Don't
be afraid," Jesus said with a
smile, "It's me! Go and tell my
disciples that I will meet them
in Galilee."

49

The Empty Tomb

John 20:2-18

Mary Magdalene found Simon
Peter and said, "The Lord has
risen! The tomb is empty!" Peter
had to see it with his own eyes.
He immediately got up and
ran toward the tomb. Another
disciple went with him and got
there before Peter. But he was
too afraid to go inside. So Peter
went in first. Jesus wasn't there!
The only thing he saw was a
folded pile of linen that Jesus'
body had been wrapped with.
The other disciple finally came
inside too. He saw the empty
tomb and believed. The two of
them went back to tell the other
disciples. It was true! Jesus had
risen!

Jesus Appears to the Disciples

John 20:19; Luke 24:37-45; John 20:21-23

The disciples were afraid of the leaders of Israel. They didn't want to be killed like Jesus. So they hid out in a room and locked the door. While they were sitting there, Jesus appeared before them! "Hello, friends," he said. But the disciples thought he was a ghost. They huddled together and clung to each other's arms. "Why are you afraid of me?" Jesus asked them. "Don't you see my wounds?"

Jesus showed his wrists where the nails had been. "It is you, Lord!" they answered in surprise.

"Do you have something to eat?" Jesus asked. One of the disciples handed him a piece of baked fish, and he ate it. Then he said, "The Father sent me to earth. But my time is over. Now I am sending you." He breathed on the disciples and said, "Receive the Holy Spirit. If you forgive anyone's sins, they will be forgiven. But if you don't, then they won't be forgiven."

Thomas Touches Jesus' Wounds

John 20:24-29

One of the twelve disciples had not seen Jesus. Thomas was not in the room with the other disciples. So they went to him and said, "We have seen the Lord!" But Thomas didn't believe them. "I must see Jesus' wounds myself and touch them with my own fingers. Then I will believe you." A week later all twelve disciples were together again in one room. They locked the door. But Jesus appeared to them just like he had before. He went over to Thomas. "Here, touch

my scars. It's me!" Jesus said. So Thomas took Jesus' hands and touched his wounds. "You are my Lord!" Thomas replied. He was happy to see Jesus again. But Jesus asked him, "Why did you doubt me? The ones who believe without seeing are the blessed ones."

A Net Full of Fish

John 21:1-14

Jesus appeared to his disciples a third time.

Peter wanted to go fishing on the lake. So the other disciples said, "We'll go with you." But the entire day and night they didn't catch even one fish. Early the next morning Jesus stood waiting for them on the shore. The disciples saw him from the boat, but they didn't realize it was Jesus. "Have you caught anything?" Jesus asked them. "No," they answered. Jesus told them to let their nets down on the other side of their boat. The disciples decided it wouldn't hurt to try. They could hardly believe their eyes as they watched the nets fill with tons of huge fish! The nets were so heavy that the disciples huffed and puffed as they were pulling them in. Peter realized it was Jesus and jumped out of the boat to swim to him while the others rowed to shore.

Jesus was waiting for them next to a small fire. He had some bread and some fish cooking over the flames. "Bring over your catch," Jesus called to them. "Let's have some break-fast!" The disciples recognized Jesus. But they didn't dare say anything. Jesus handed a piece of bread and some fish to each one of the disciples. Then they ate together.

56

Jesus and Peter
John 21:15-19

After Jesus and his disciples finished eating, Jesus asked Peter a question. "Do you love me more than the others?"

"Yes Lord, you know I do!" Peter answered.

"Good," Jesus replied. "Then take care of my sheep."

Jesus asked him a second time, "Do you love me?"

Again Peter answered, "Yes Lord, you know I love you!"

"Then take care of my sheep," Jesus said.

Jesus asked Peter a third time, "Do you really love me?"

Peter's feelings were hurt. He

thought Jesus doubted his love. But he answered, "Lord you know everything. You know I love you."

"Good," Jesus replied. "Then feed my sheep and follow me!"

Jesus asked Peter if he loved him three times, just as many times as Peter had denied him. He wanted to make sure Peter was ready to be his follower again.

Jesus Returns to God

Acts 1:3-11

Jesus stayed with his disciples forty days after he had risen from the grave. He spoke about the kingdom of God with them. He also told them, "Stay in Jerusalem until the Father gives you the Holy Spirit. John baptized you with water, but in a few days God will baptize you with his Spirit." The disciples had a lot of questions for Jesus. "Are you going to give us a king?" they asked. But Jesus said, "Don't worry about those things. They are in God's hands. But the Holy Spirit will give you power. Spread the news and tell everyone in the world about me!" Then Jesus went up to heaven in a cloud.

Long after Jesus had disappeared, the disciples still stood staring up in awe at the sky. An angel stood next to them smiling. "What are you looking at?" he asked. The disciples glanced over at the angel in surprise. Then the angel said, "Jesus is in heaven now! But he will come back someday. And he will come the same way that you saw him go."

61

The Contemporary Bible Series